THIS BEING EDEN

Roger Caldwell

PETERLOO POETS

First published in 2001
by Peterloo Poets
The Old Chapel, Sand Lane, Calstock, Cornwall PL18 9QX, U.K.

© 2001 by Roger Caldwell

A catalogue record for this book is available
from the British Library

ISBN 1-871471-88-5

Printed in Great Britain by
Antony Rowe Ltd, Chippenham, Wilts.

THIS BEING EDEN

ACKNOWLEDGEMENTS

Acknowledgements are due to the editors of the following magazines in which versions of many of these poems first appeared: *Ariel, Chapman, Envoi, Haiku Quarterly, Journal of Contemporary Anglo-Scandinavian Poetry, Lines Review, New Statesman, Orbis, Outposts, Philosophy Now, Poetry New Zealand, Poetry Scotland, Poetry Wales, Quartz, Rialto, Swansea Review, Wascana Review.*

'Poets: An Endangered Species' first appeared in *Sing Freedom!* (Faber & Faber)

south west arts

for Alexander,
with apologies

Contents

1.

The Fortunate Fall

We were never turned away – we left, my Lord,
the garden of our own accord.

The serpent spoke to Eve. Eve spoke to me.
We talked in the shadow of the tree.

Lord, did you doubt our hands would reach
to grab the knowledge that you would not teach

of all life's secrets? Lord, we loved you less
when you gazed strangely on our nakedness.

You gave us dominion, Lord. But now we know
it was to do the work that you should do,

and we've learned the price of it – it was your breath
of life which also brought us death.

In the sloughed skin of the snake I see
an immortality denied to me.

You washed your hands of dust, Lord. Now you brood,
exiled to Eden, and to solitude.

Urwald

Our island ancestors
who knew their world,

enclosed by dangerous forest
and surrounded by a treacherous sea,

was an interval of light
between two hostile winters

found civilization in the mead-halls
and a clutch of simple homesteads

in the wood's brief clearing,
felt no need to be alone

when loneliness was all around.
We who know no landscape

uncluttered with man's artifacts
seek comfort in what's alien, blind,

find solace only
in what our ancestors found most to fear

– by entering their imagined
vanished dense dark woods.

The Epigoni

The birds that sing in the garden are
notated by Messiaen. The clouds

which scud across the sky are there
by grace of Constable. Human voices

all around descant on what were
natural things. A faded Coca-Cola can

on top of the bus-shelter close
to Woolwich Arsenal station has become

by inadvertence almost natural in dearth
of what was nature once. We're epigoni,

footnotes to the Ur-text, footnotes indeed
to footnotes, words unread by God, until,

reversing time, escaping entropy, a bird,
fledgling, flies from out the canvas, clouds

ascend from flute to piccolo to blue beyond
and, upside down a moment's space, the bird

hangs precarious from a lesser cloud,
and the mind's not tempted to reduce the scene

to its own design, no words are formed
to say what only words can say, the can's

lost liquor then to artificial throats
gives promise of a natural drink,

the epigoni flee in awe of Adam.

Hobbesian Poem

Our "words so many counters"
and the heart a spring,
each nerve itself
a sort of string,
each joint a wheel
to give us motion.

If we are, then,
machines that feel,
the poems that we make
are computations
not bound in any way by truth,
but a counting out of images
from a memory decayed,
and freedom is a stone
flung by a boy

— a stone that thinks
the best of joy
is to reach the limit
so described
by its own parabola.

The Dummy Speaks

I am my own ventriloquist: the strings
move too much the master to let master say

that he is in control. I cut, inglorious,
his comic capers, then, collapsed into a box,

I hear his paralytic wit without me
expatiate too broadly on a theme

itself too narrow. Subject, object, I am too
his modus vivendi, audience's *joie de vivre*,

have more of nature in me, being so contrived
better of wood and wires than he of flesh and bone.

Comedian, his patter down the haunted halls
has nothing of his own that's worthy to express:

I speak through him – he does not speak through me.
He's my automaton, invention, and his life

is not worth living that's not also mine.
Check-suited fool, death's entertainer,

does he think, when he's alone, I am no better
than the wire-pulled god he made in his own image?

Cervantes

Don Quixote and his Pancha
travel on
even when the book is closed.

Although the products of his brain
live on in us
Cervantes' sleep is not disturbed.

He lies as still as those anonymous
beneath green turf,
mere undulations in the ground.

It's how one lives one's life that counts
and death the fact
that once one had a life to lead.

If my dead father comes into my dreams
he's scarcely grateful
for the visit – any more than is

Cervantes when we enter his.

Scene from 'David Copperfield'

In some Victorian tavern David sits,
young, intense and tousled-haired,

drinking in the old man's words
with their tang of the sea and dialect

rehearsed from a discarded phrase-book,
keeps an anxious eye on (one without desire)

the youthful sole-eyed prostitute
consumptive at the door, pure-hearted, looking in.

He's very much the gentleman
with fashionable top-hat, silk scarf

flung careless on the peg above him.
He knows whose story he is in,

that in the end all three will prosper.
Outside an unfamiliar London lies

for those who sit at an adjacent table
and are not mentioned in the chapter,

who, when we empty our last glass and leave,
are left anonymous to wander

with no words to guide us through the fog
to home or to a happy ending.

Leaving for Lambarene

1.
It's time to leave the village,
cross the bridge by the stream
where the children would chase

Mausche the Jew on his donkey-cart.
Time to leave too the Kayserberg Castle
in the shadow of which you entered the world,

the mountains, the woods,
the church where you watched
swallows gather for their journey south.

Time to wait again at the station
for the single-track train to crawl,
snail-slow, all the length of the valley,

then puff onward to Colmar,
for the Strasburg connection
and Paris express. It's time to say:

"I have loved the castles of Alsace."

2.
The statue of the brooding negro
gigantic in the Champs de Mars
had brought you far to find

tsetse by day, mosquito by night,
life and death in the jungle mission.
For now and forever it will be,

on a piano out-of-tune and damaged
by rat-urine, Bach thumped out
four-square to equatorial darkness;

cicadas and lepers; bellows
of hippopotamus; a world which played
the fool with reverence for life.

               "Ogange – fetish-man,
               papa pour nous, papa pour nous,
               we owe him to Lord Jesus.

               "He told the doctor and his wife
               to come to the Ogowe
               and to cure sick negroes."

3.
Outdated, racist
scalpel-wielding saint,
you never learned the languages

of those you called your "younger" brothers.
You never sat with them at table.
You played at God. God's played with you

now ogange – fetish-man – is dead.
Your Christ died too for a mistake.
The indifferent Ogowe flows

still out to sea. Within a jungle clearing
Albert and Hélène lie side by side
beneath two crosses, and together

as they so rarely were in life.
The worm's coiled in the heart, and turned.
In the leaving once for Lambarene

is something that redeems the rest.

Americas

"How far can one go in the extermination of meaning? ...
Aim for the point of no return. That is the key." (Jean
Baudrillard, *America*)

One can make anything a poem. One can
make anyone a person. It needs but the stamp
of an authority. Imprimatur of God
made Adam man – till Adam questioned it.
Along the freeway, past its suicide motels
I sought the vanishing point. My travelling
extinguished names, put zeroes after zero,
      added desert to the desert.

I'd been Arctic weather, that I knew,
in downtown Hamilton, cold as ice I'd walked
on Lake Ontario. I looked at the world
through crooked lenses, seeking signs
in cloud-formations, women's hair, or notes
discarded, torn across, and hostages to fate
in lonely trash-cans, heaps of leaves when fall
      arrived without the mailman.

We were hand in hand, America and I,
one time. Yet someone with a southern drawl
beyond mid-western ditches, fields of corn,
was between a promise and an absence.
The nigger geese when silent when we spoke
in whispers in the bayou. Did we have to fight
the Battle of New Orleans? You are miles
      distant, I am years away.

My Americas. Everyone's Americas.
I played along the railroad like a child,
all kinds of weed sprang up. What carrier wind
blew down across the continent, brought
discord there? No cacti in Death Valley, dawn
in Adeline, no railroad shack. We never danced
in moonlight. Catfish never came. No point
except the point of no return.

One can make anything a poem, one can't
make anyone a person. Cramped and damp
in Surrey, England, I wind old-style clocks
as lights go out. Like a child to an old house,
too frightened to do cartwheels, I return
in moonlight now, without authority, and knock
gently on the door of distant lost impossible
                Americas, and need no answer.

Niagaras

1.
After years of – if not searching –
waiting, then, through ice-cold nights,
inconsequent tomorrows,

to find that this was what awaited us
since someone, something
had betrayed our trust

means – or what else could it mean? –
the waiting's over by the waterfall
and meaning lost.

2.
He thought he'd worried out at last
beyond the wasted words
something which made sense in spite of them

though, when a gust of wind sent snow
so cold it must have travelled from Niagara,
beliefs he'd held, long thought absurd

in memory, flashed an instant true
and he stumbled out into a day
now turned from grey to icy-new,

and was glad to shake off meaning
though uncertain for how long
could confidence in nothing be maintained.

3.
What's left, then, to reply on? Why rely
on anything at all? Even oneself
of whom one claimed

a nodding acquaintanceship with once
is off elsewhere, and though I see
there's someone crossing a tightrope

who might fall – or not – it's someone other
than the person I awoke to years ago.
And sure as one is one, and two were two

the voice with which we'd each bemoan
or celebrate his fall into the icy rapids
– that's someone else's voice now too.

4.
What kind of trust was it, and who
was honoured in the seeming
to be natural? If we were actors on the scene

acting stilled into a pose
before a frozen waterfall, with camera after.
The drops still fresh upon our brows

we now find were imagined things
even when the sun shone through,
turned snow to watery paradise.

Past our imaginings
the water fell, and I fell too.
Winter turned the droplets back to ice.

Wittgenstein in Glasgow

Say, there are basilisks as much
as there is V.A.T., and words
– words enough to say that words
are at least as insufficient as
the world in which there are no words
beyond the kailyard.

Some people too are less than words
- I won't name names that only
name themselves, since I myself
have felt myself a comma or a hyphen
off the page, and sensed not seen
a row of asterisks whirl by.

Today it's otherwise, for,
walking down Argyle Street
on a leaner than usual Tuesday
and far from home, my farmyard fowl
have come to roost, however briefly,
not as verbs or nouns but in a world
that has no need of names except to say
Buchanan Street or *Universe*, another
time and place.

                  Neuronal man,
not minding p's or q's, I let
the crowd around me mingle with myselves
likewise moving down the thoroughfare,
not cut-throat nor cut-price, but making
purchases upon the grammar of a life,
seeking signs that now might read:
Mother Carey's Chickens, Pembrokeshire Potatoes.
in preparation for the next fat Wednesday.

To Joe, from Another Country

And there will be, no doubt,
the drag queens on the Boulevard Saint Germain
in all their flouncing glory, seasonal
as bluebells in the Vienna woods, reliable
as tax returns. But Joe, you won't be there,
or here, or anywhere to watch
the barman pull another pint, eyes wide
and blue, betraying tough-man pose
with Glaswegian growl conceived in Edinburgh.

When the ice cracked on the Neva
you were some days dead; you never heard
– who'd never listen – it was Time had called,
last orders taken. You would not allow
the failure of your body to submit
to all your petty tyrannies. And, Joe,
you turned aside enquiries with a joke,
met death midday with an unfinished glass.

If you found winter in the spring
you couldn't blame the season. For the earth itself,
through eons, knows a lengthening day in which
there are more shadows cast.
                              We drain,
survivors for a while, a glass in memory, and then,
in glaring sun, go out to join the slow cortège
to a place you would not grant existed.

Teheran Before the Revolution

The carpet-sellers on the Avenue Firdowsi
– But there are no carpets, and there are no stalls.
And there is no Avenue Firdowsi. Every city

builds on the ruins of another city.
The key you have will open the apartment door
to the next but last. My London windows

watch the Moscow workers swarm across the square,
release the rich and long-contained aromas,
from nights in Herat, of sweet Afghan gold,

stale fumes of German beer from Hanover.
But the sun is dirty yellow down the morning streets
and someone shouts "The Shah is dead". I'm lost

to the quiet oasis of myself in Russell Square,
then hear faint gun-fire till November rain
means dampened wood-piles and failed squibs.

Who was it sheltered in a westernized hotel,
drank beer, and smoked a nervous cigarette,
exited to autumn heat, a city burning?

They did that day what England did in effigy.
Unruly in the Shah's time, down the alleyway,
she lifted her chador, showed nakedness beneath.

London is my Teheran. I step into a shady hall
out of the glare: old *Der Spiegel*'s line a dusty floor,
and fallen photographs. Lost to claims of history,

the sleeper's heavy breathing from the curtained room
when the giant cockroach of the Middle East
clambers across his dreams gives out no hint

that he'll awaken to a city full of baby's cries
out of the range of gunfire. Child-like himself,
he sleeps the heavier for a city that is lost

to half-forgotten faces turned against the sun,
the carpet-sellers and the crowds, the whirring fan
– not stilled - of Teheran before the Revolution.

2.

Conspirators

My pale conspirator – I met him in the mirror,
traced his black moustache on pallid features, I
rehearsing life before him naked.

Yet he's killed so many down the years – as much
by inadvertence as bravado. Nonetheless
this is a pact I can't renege from

turn it as I will, my guilty secret, my bravura
always in his image, though he looked through me
most when I looked up at him

secure in his malevolence as I could never be.
My model and my *cri de coeur*, when mirrors shatter
he will be my memory of mirrors,

will remain what were the splinters of my fate,
his thin-lipped smile betraying words which faltered
on my lips against his certainties.

I reached up a left hand to touch his right,
but it was always I who flinched away.
His laugh is silent when I leave

for a world outside beyond the reach of mirrors
– blind, opaque – and gracelessly seek out
our long-agreed-on sorry assignations.

The Body-Mind Problem

I've had about me longer than I'd own
this thing of flesh, of blood, of bone,

and a changing face I think would fit
anyone who made a claim on it.

What is this heavy-breathing thing
that makes a joke of love, and lovemaking?

The substance I am, and which lurks inside,
has its own, and not a body's pride.

Or, when I listen to Bach's B Minor Suite,
does an ageing carcass still tap out the beat?

Did ten fumbling fingers play the notes
on which my stranded spirit dotes?

If I lost a finger or a toe
would a little piece of mind then go?

I cannot own, or understand
what links me through the pineal gland.

The best for body mind can yet discover
is to make the one a symbol of the other.

But my tormentor's long grown wise
to such time-honoured strategies

and finds the mind with its aspiring thought
a wayward germ the body's caught,

proclaiming infinity and spreading lies
– the disease of which the body dies.

The Air of Another Planet

Thus walke I, lyk a restless kaityff
And on the ground, which is my modres gate,
I knokke with my staf, bothe erly and late,
And seye 'Leeve moder, leet me in!'
(Chaucer, *The Pardoner's Tale*)

No, this is not the world I knew
when locked up in a better place
scarcely knowing I was I.

The sounds, the colours
of another world
drew me to my fall.

I was all in all. I should have stayed,
curled in my darkness,
enjoying the heartbeat

but they threw me out
to alien weather, alien people
never kith and kin of mine.

I lay there and I longed
to be tipped out to darkness,
– how was I to know

they'd cheat me with another planet?
I have no peace in such a place,
its very air

thickens in my lungs.
I've had enough of light.
Let me return

to the only home I ever knew,
enjoying the heartbeat, alone
and in the dark forever.

Mother, let me in again.

Ostriches

"Like the ostrich, I cannot fly, yet I have wings that
give me that feeling of flight." (Coleridge)

Ostriches through evolution
have kept their wings, but cannot use them

– in consequence of which they must
use legs to cross the desert dust,

and can run fast, outrun the rest
of mammals who think legs are best.

Nonetheless when ostriches dream
they return to an ancestral theme

of wings that soar, reach up so high
to a cloudless, brighter, better sky

– of the ostrich as he really is,
aloft, and knowing happiness.

But when they wake, poor foolish things,
flex in vain their silly wings.

Judas: His Apology

It could have been any of the Twelve.
One of them at least there had to be
who must act Judas, have the taste to do
that wicked thing, fulfil God's plan.
If I, Escariot, was the man,
and if it was required He be betrayed,
for that a betrayer was required too.

By acting Judas I saved someone else
who's grinning at me now in heaven,
and who lacked all courage for the deed.
I saved the Saviour who, without my help,
could never save the world. No Judas kiss,
no cross. No cross, and then God's Son
would have shirked the burden of the Father.
Legions of angels were at His command.

And it was prophesied of the Twelve,
in the new age, that each would rule
over a twelfth part of the earth.
In days when prophecies are fulfilled
I'll claim my share, will have my realm,
– perhaps the most populous of all –
of zealots, hypocrites and fools
who, at first surprised, will find it apt
once they've come to know themselves
(and they'll have time enough)
that they have entered Judas' Kingdom.

Bad Weather for Some

"Glattes Eis
Ein Paradeis
Für den, der gut zu tanzen weiss."
(Nietzsche)

Going out today seemed perilous
– though no snow as yet, too many signs

of winter's presence to give comfort –
and everywhere abroad were stories

of persons strangled by their own silk scarves
suddenly frozen in the zero weather,

of clothes stuck fast to bodies so
they couldn't be removed without removing skin,

the ice so slippery, so densely-packed
someone stepping out to close his gate

had skated out into another country
fast, but yet not fast enough

to stop air freezing in his lungs,
they found his corpse down a lane in Shropshire

features stiffened in his first surprise
though at ninety-three he'd little left to live for

and was therefore one of the luckier ones.
Another was stabbed by a falling icicle

his body taken as refrigerated meat
and used as food by starving villagers

– Hearing tales such as these
I trembled behind the faded chintz

for what seemed years
in a chilly room, listening to Rachmaninov

beneath a bare dim bulb
till cold had made the ceiling crack,

then decided I had had enough,
would go out to my doom if doom it was

with threadbare overcoat and missing glove
and underwear designed for warmer climates,

so singing my improvised Te Deum
softly underneath my breath

went out to that forbidden zone
beyond the doorstep and the garden-gnomes

but found the air so balmy, mild
spring-like where no one else would walk

I could as happily have travelled naked.

Say It With Flowers

Then I shall say it with flowers,
proclaim it in wreaths and bouquets.

I shall scent it with sweet belladonna.
With sudden spikes of gladioli

I shall belabour the point.
With the brief nocturnal flower of Cereus,

with thick clusters of spines,
with fly-traps, with henbane

I'll drive the point home.
And not only with flowers

but with poison éclairs, assorted rum trifles
with a whole bag of sweet sticky confections

I'll expatiate upon my theme.
As with a laser beam I'll pencil out

in letters etched upon the heart,
venomously strange, of pure white light,

this message too of earthly love
which seems to say as much: *I hate you.*

The Hoarder

Travel light – of course I would
if there were anywhere that I could go.

I'd simplify
if there were a core from which to strip away.

It seems instead that to subtract
is to end up as a minus number.

No wonder then for stay-at-homes
to not discard a single shred's

the better part of wisdom
where no wisdom's known

so when there is an interlude
one may pick and choose at will,

but sure as one goes through the pile
of unfulfilled intentions

half-forgotten vows
one finds as all along the way

too much of what one wanted least
too little that one really loved.

Limits

On the other side of joy
your pulse slows down
each ray of light is held transfixed
Bach lasts years
and is a silence at the heart of things.

On the farther side of joy
you heed no limits
having travelled on
beyond emotional extremes
beyond weight and measures
and the apparatus of loving.
And the universe will dance
on a pinpoint.

On the farthest side of joy
there is no knowing.
No one breathes.
The farthest side of joy
is more than words can say.

This side of joy
we dance on clumsy feet
Bach is twenty minutes
played with fumbling fingers
Bach is just warped plastic
and a battered score.

This side of joy
humanity is swine
we all discuss
minutest variations of the swill
and love is when two snouts meet
happiness the mating of a boar and sow
– our poets, swinish sentimental,
grunt their porcine ardours.

Oh, but one must learn one's limits
and try a limited love like ours
and be content with bits and pieces
shadows, shells
and hints of silence.

Left-Handed

Left-handed, that I always was
which, I soon found, was sinister.

Following a virtuous teacher
I formed laborious letters with my right,
which I did badly, though she praised,
as if it were my best, imperfect scrawl,
encouraged what I did least well.

She only taught me subterfuge.
Behind her back, no circus animal,
I did what to me was natural,
thereby earned her praises more.

But that in secret I could only do
left-handed what in public with my right
I knew to be inadequate
taught me only that, to tell the truth,
it is necessary first to learn to lie.

Images

Tired of being misunderstood
I made a model of myself from wood,

added a pinch of skin for verisimilitude
and a handful of bones the dog had chewed,

clockwork motors to move limbs
and a computerized larynx to sing hymns,

simulated tear-ducts and glass eyes,
painted upraised eyebrows to suggest surprise,

set the thing together with fast-setting glue,
looked at my creation, hoped that it would do,

made thus for all the world to see
an image which resembled me.

The trick's done wonders. All the same,
to hear the world address him in my name,

to see those flock to him who fled from me
praising mere mechanical ingenuity,

I wonder, travelling the world about
in secret, having let my monster out,

if all the others likewise have saved face
by setting painted clockwork figures in their place,

and hidden their true selves away
so only simulacra see the light of day

until in time each feels within
that it's he is artificial, and the image genuine.

The Other

I wasn't aware of him at first,
my erring twin, but later I learned
he went off the rails at an early age
and prowls around the world whilst I
lead a dull but spotless life at home.
He scorns me and my kind, I'm told,
mocks where I choose to acquiesce,
will come to no good end, I fear,
who, for all that he's as old as I am,
has never learned what growing up's about.
I should like to come to terms with him,
this roaring boy who haunts me so,
help him, as a brother, to see sense.
But my task would be a simpler one
if there weren't as well a ghostly third
who, having no character of his own,
constantly judges and compares
and, as from a superior posture,
speaks coldly of our lives, declares
no merit's to be found in either.

Chinese Walls

Walls which keep the others out,
barbarians, intruders, serve
also to contain ourselves.

What lies beyond the walls?
outsiders ask, not knowing
that the palace like a house of cards
protected from the merest breeze
is nothing solid.

Like them I'm walking round and round
probing where the weakness lies,
sniffing my bouquet of secrets.

These are Chinese walls
containing other walls. Beyond
there's nothing possible to grasp or hold
that doesn't disappear between one's fingers,
dissolve into the empty air
like a forgotten promise.

Nothing to gain by scaling them
or breaking down. You'd only find
the wilderness outside had met
the wilderness within.

Neighbours

That there is evil in the world
is manifest, else there is no good.

I see it in my neighbour's eye
that he intends no good to me.

To love my neighbour would be love
of that which does myself most harm.

To hate him, on the other hand,
would make more evil than exists.

I therefore shall embrace,
as far as I can, indifference,

not wishing him other than he is,
not wishing him anything at all,

and try to think he is not there,
no monstrous presence through the wall,

though knowing, if he dies in pain
of a long incurable disease,

he will think more deeply on his sins
and I more deeply God is just.

At Number Seventeen

"For what is Christendom? It is a continual
reduction of the price, from generation to
generation, of calling oneself a Christian."
(Kierkegaard)

It's known throughout St Margaret's Banks:
At Number Seventeen they're Christians.

They go church on Sundays, that's to say,
he's in the choir, she irons his surplices

singing hymns, no doubt, the while,
their boys two little spiteful monsters.

From they way they talk, they dress
you'd think them products of another era.

Yet what's to claim Christian in times like these
if it's not to have the vices all have

plus hypocrisy and sanctimoniousness?
He with his grave bald dome and nervous tic,

she with pursed tight lips, thin smile
and Fifties polyester frock

– one wonders what Christ himself would think
could he return, past martyrdoms

and nineteen centuries of blood, to see
all hard-fought battles come to this:

prim, small-minded and ridiculous.

3.

Kicking Leaves

An odd memory of my kicking leaves
close by a river that I can't locate

recurs – and, too, with each recurrence
I remember the bridge over which we walked,

then my face pressed hard against the gate
of the drive to the house we didn't visit,

and leaves again, golden and damp
thick under my feet – this and no more:

the abiding images, the same emotion,
distant, of feeling both happy and lost.

You'd think after all these years
I would also remember the time and place

and also the person I was with,
but I don't, and accept that I'll never know,

through not ungrateful when the scene returns
of myself as maybe I never was

it seems as good as companionless
in a foreign place, and idly kicking leaves.

The Missing Piece

As a child I did the puzzle once.
Next time around a piece was missing.

The gap betrayed the grand design,
made all my efforts come to nothing.

I searched and searched for that missing piece
till I grew up, forgot. Years later,

on a visit to my mother's house,
I found it when the search was over

lodged behind a skirting-board,
the puzzle it had once belonged to

long since discarded with my other toys.
The single piece meant nothing now,

had nothing in particular to tell
except it had belonged to something,

was the solution, had it not been lost,
to a problem not perhaps worth solving.

In My Mother's House

Here in this house
among my mother's things
I cannot rest.

Yet when she dies
these cards, these few small souvenirs,
this taste in furniture
not me, my sisters
will be all her life was.

So too, myself.
The mass of papers never say
what the mind thought,
how I lived.
And the clothes in the wardrobe
fit the average body.

And who'd be comfortable in my house
if they couldn't disregard
the junk I've left, throw out
memorials to lost solitude
unmeaning now?

Refusal to Write

It's an ideal night in which to write a poem
– no noise from neighbours, baby

is in bed, wife watching television,
I am not drunk and have no pressing worries:

here, if at any time, the words should flow.
Instead there is an absence

when the mind stops, is a pause between
two ticks of the clock, between the whirrs

of the the great machine, where nothing happens,
a stillness that no words can say.

I have no need, and shall not try to say it,
this neither elation nor despair

though there's something beckons
that is not poetry or love

or anything to make a cliché of.
This is a call which needs no answers.

God winds the clocks up, and the Devil
dozes with his engines off.

Poets: an Endangered Species

The death of Lorca worries me.
Why did they need to gun him down?

Not for being Red, or a *maricón*
but because he was a poet, and wrote poetry

in an iron age of civil war.
Mandelstam likewise.

He threw a squib in Stalin's eyes.
That wasn't what they killed him for:

his ironies of inner life
were insupportable to a state

built on fanaticism, hate,
suspicion. He knew well enough

to play the holy fool
in iron times was death:

he died each time he drew his breath.
What these learned in a harder school

than ours, we learn from history
that can't repeat itself as such

but doesn't scorn sequels overmuch.
The death of Lorca worries me.

Sandcastles

The king was always an usurper. It was
the dirty-faced rascal who had all the rights.

We saw it fall, the castle. It was built to fall.
The sea filled up its moat. High ramparts

tottered with the rising tide. The shells,
mere decoration, slipped from sliding walls.

The king hid trembling for misplaced ambition
lonely in his last room left. The rascal,

before the sea could make its last assault,
flattened the creation with a savage spade.

I am my father now. I am my failed king.
Canute-like, watch the waves roll in

and out again. Oblivious, my son
seeks new conquests on a plundered beach.

Ivinghoe Beacon

We trod the Downs as bare-kneed children,
danced, pranced along the Ridgeway where
our prehistoric ancestors had trudged.
Ivinghoe Beacon, and hot sun burned down.

A camel caravan across the Afghan desert;
pre-Revolution Teheran – the same hot sun.
An air-cooled library in Hamilton. In Hanover
a loving couple, nude, strolled down the Bahnhofstrasse.

I lay the map across my knee; it's yellowed
under sunlight's glare, displays a path
back into the past across a future. Mine. Mine too
the memories of twisting lanes, the rug,

the sandwiches, the sun, the broken thermos-flask.
Glass in our orange-juice. Dry-mouthed
we dined among lost ancestors. Parched lips
know no soft sibilants of old Celtic tongue.

Mother of my friend was African. Spoke Xhosa.
I remember the aberrant word I traced
in schoolboy cursive on a misted pane.
Ghosts on a paleolithic path. What Oxford drawl

now gives answer to a child's voice? In Africa
my friend grows middle-aged. The villages round Tring
know motor-bikes; helmetless their riders snarl
through Hertfordshire, hair plastered back with rain.

We bring back booty from another land. We make
our own museums of ourselves. Who were
the barbaroi? Who walked the Ridgeway then?
Cracked shaving-mirror only shows

a stateless face, and lips frame words
from self-constructed lexicon. We saw
six counties from the Beacon. Shards of glass
lie buried deep in prehistoric soil.

Much-travelled Odysseus returned, all but
companionless, to Ithaca. I too
was in a foreign country, found my own way back,
one of a group, dry from the long day's outing.

Islas Encantadas

"an archipelago of aridities without
inhabitant, history or hope of either"
(Herman Melville)

1.
Further than Americas – though Coca-Coca cans
will fade among the rusted muskets left
by eighteenth-century misanthropic anchorites.
Plunder from old pirate-ships: uncaring,
lazy iguanas stroll over heaps of lost doubloons.
The spiders weave their webs and wait.
Chas. Darwin, Christian gent, along these shores
where God was exiled, found a garden
never known by Adam. Slow, beneath volcanic dust,
a creature crawls who will be one day man.

2.
I carry my briefcase in my hand,
walk respectable down Chipstead Valley Road
and turn the corner, find that wind has dropped,
face blue empty seas, feel wet sand rise up
between my newly-naked toes. God knows
what's washed up with the tides round Purley
or giant squid is stranded on the shoals
of Kingswood, what weird primeval bird in Tadworth
flexes wings to fly. I write all day
in safe Victorian sentences and hope I do no harm.

3.

Flightless cormorants, crabs that scuttled
on the back of lizards. A child in Hertfordshire,
I dug for archaeopteryx in clayey soil.
Adult, I cross the Thames each day, am seeking signs.
I shan't go fishing on the downs, or gather
seaweed in the hills. There pirates fashioned benches
for a beauty-spot who'd kill men with a curse
for sixpence. The only snakes non-venomous;
no carnivores, no predators save owl and buzzard.
They knew no sabbath. Whose was the observing eye?

4.

I'm trying out my own new species. Venus'
fly-trap in a pot, fresh from Carolina, is
the cynosure of my son's eyes.
It looked a dying thing, in foreign climates,
then enticed, and closed its spiny fingers round,
and throttled quite, a late-October tired
English wasp. My island-volcano has collapsed
in on itself. I stay, know evolution
even from such small things as this.
And everywhere abroad are islands.

Crossroads

1.

Alone, in bed-sitting rooms, or gone
between two books for a stroll in the park
the industrious scholar thinks he knows
what loneliness is, sees people so
lost in isolation, thinks
how far apart from one another
all are, each in his inviolable castle
with the drawbridge up.

       And when, with drawbridge down,
marries, acquires children, neighbours
learns how wide the moat is:
Intimacies no bridge can span.

2.

Nearly middle-aged, and nearly respectable,
with my briefcase I board the morning train.
Alongside drowsy commuters, I recall the time
– opium in Moscow, journey to Herat –
when I was a vagrant through the world
or thought myself such, if I thought at all,
but not the inner exile that I now am,
wonder: *When I did such things*
was I part in England, telling my story,
just as I now am most abroad, enjoying
foreign adventures as my train draws in,
belated, to Victoria Station?

3.
Remembering to put the rubbish out
– one of life's simple petty tasks.
Tying the inadequate black plastic bag
inexpert with a piece of string
and hauling the bundle to the road
for cats and foxes to attack by night,
releasing empty lager-cans,
cigar-stumps and prawn-curry packets
discarded manuscripts, old shoes,
for neighbours to stare at, when my brain
that aches for leisure and philosophy
free of all life's detritus
is left here too to rot

                    –Ah, but then philosophers as well
must sometimes have had to put rubbish out
first having pondered on what rubbish is,
since the most complex of philosophies
also connect with petty simple things.

4.
"Lächeln wir nicht auch, wenn die Kinder weinen?"
(Kleist)

Our child's laments, however loud
and disproportionate in a parent's ear
to the disturbance which occasioned them
are heartfelt, are genuine enough
though, knowing how much more in life
there is to cry about, we adults smile
at his small miseries, uneasily aware
that God might likewise, when we sorrow and despair
of obvious injustices and life gone wrong,
suppress a secret and superior smile at ours.

5.
I didn't want to recover those scenes,
long forgotten, of childhood when I wailed
in an unforgiving parent's ear for things
never worth the having, but to travel on
free of such lumber

      –Yet with my own child's
small persistent hand at my reluctant sleeve
learn I must go back so he can travel forward.

6.
I saw the cottage first. and then the garden
tempted me to linger, something from the past
– old English flowers, the foxgloves, hollyhocks,
the old man pruning roses, white-haired wife
both oblivious of me as I watched,
enjoying the taste of rural life and peace
for as long as my four-year son could stand
already impatient at my wrist, and thought:

Would she and I, in thirty years, our life's work done,
manage too some quiet self-contented idyll,
knowing what our lives had been, what memories
would also be? – And was our future this, with luck,
conventionally rustic and conventionally dull,
among the foxgloves and the hollyhocks?

Summer Night in Rochester

The windows open, summer come,
sleepless, I listen to the trains
rumble their way through Rochester
to some not very distant destination.

Well past eleven – and the drunks
totter, noisy, from the nearby pub
towards a destination nearer still
where they may lay down heavy heads
and hope that beery breath
turns sweeter by tomorrow morning.

All think they're going somewhere,
England, summer, this weekend,
and I, to all appearance motionless,
think too I'm somehow on my way,
though to another place, I trust,
not told too clearly in advance,
but better than I fear it is.

Andorra or The Curious Thing

In noonday heat we rested by the stream.
She washed cherries in the cool clear water,
laid them on leaves spread on the stones.
I admired her Japanese precision
in Andorra once.

We talked through a lazy afternoon,
I bad French, she oriental Spanish.
Once having known pure Pyrennean streams
we won't taste others.

It disturbed me that I thought of Eden then,
too conscious that this was an idyll.
Named, it should be in a book, portrayed
for those who never knew that once
they lived in Eden.

It should be ruined by such knowingness.
We all sense, when the page is turned,
what time's twist of fate will bring,
how, to sophisticates, a new breeze blows
from a diseased Parnassus.

Outside Andorra our two lives
in separate streams are far removed
from what we knew as idyll then.
But nothing of it's stained or ruined – that's
the curious thing.

This Being Eden

There was, it is true,
a garden of sorts – and a tree
of a kind our science deemed impossible:
we were not tempted by its shrivelled fruits.

There was a path as well
where two had trod – the naked toes
and stubborn heels were clear,
imprinted in dried mud, and showed
no hurry on that journey out.

Serpents were little in evidence.
Of beauty – there were butterflies, of course,
as much as there were beetles, snails, and slugs.
The early reports, we all agreed,
had somewhat written up the scene
whose history was desolation.

In darkest moments we rehearsed
the rigours of our coming here,
the heartbreaks, shipwrecks and the cost
of having travelled out so far,
the scorn we'd meet at our return
if lacking proof we hadn't tarried
at the blissful isles we never found,
of basilisks
              – We thought it best,
this being Eden, and this time around,
remembering an exile once, to settle, try
to make a garden worthy of the wilderness.

Report on Planet 93

This is a cool and uninviting planet.
Much of it is water, and the atmosphere
is unpropitious for the growth
of intelligent life-forms. It is a world
of swirling clouds and polar ice, the air
is poisonous with nitrogen and oxygen.
The most remarkable of its indigenous
inhabitants is undoubtedly the beetle
which exists (as far as our instruments detect)
in many thousand different species,
swarms everywhere about the planet's land-mass.
There's too a curious bipedal mammal
– the signals it gave out, through various, were such
they lacked all definite significance:
we must conclude it utters sounds at random.
There is one species only, it appears.
The varieties of lichen are of academic interest
but not significant to detain us, given
the potential riches of this galaxy
and the few remaining light-years. Hence
the brevity of this report. We did not land.